Job Interview Preparation

The Ultimate Resource to Get the Job you Really Want

By Gary Cooper

Job Interview Preparation

Published in the United States by Awesome Life Resources. 2015

Ebook ASIN: B00KMWSGBQ

Paperback: 978-1507776469

Table of Contents

FREE AUDIO BOOK

Don't forget to get access to the Free Audio Book version of Job Interview Preparation by viewing the below link:

http://forms.aweber.com/form/10/1771222810.htm

Format: .mp3

Size: 21.4 mb

Duration: 01:26:29

Disclaimer

This ebook, Job Interview Preparation: The Ultimate Resource to Get the Job you Really Want, has been written with an intention of providing information to users. Although every effort has been taken to ensure validity and accuracy of information provided here, readers are requested to take immense care and precaution while using the information provided here. The authors do not take responsibility for any loss, or damages incurred as a result of following the information provided in this book.

Wishing you good luck for getting the job you really want!

Introduction

Let us face the facts; we all had to face the interview panel at least once in our lifetimes. It involves the fear of facing a group of men and women whose primary aim in life seems to be to ask you precisely those questions that you don't know the answers to! With your teacher telling you to prepare a better resume, your mentors telling you about the specific technical skills you have to bone up on, and your friends giving you 'expert' advice on the best colors to wear to the interview, you are confused and anxious about the whole interview process.

A job interview feels like the ultimate test of endurance and attitude. Although there is no sure way to know the right way to prepare for the interview process - or even to predict the outcome of interviews - you can, however, give your best in the interview so that you will be considered for the position. Your success depends solely on how you perform during the interview; how well you are able to project yourself in those few hours will lay the path to your future in the company. You should be able to relate your job experiences, education, skills, and interests with the needs of the employer. Only when you are able to convince the interviewer that you are perfect for their needs or that you can be trained to excel in the given field, will you be selected. Although a job interview can be a very intimidating experience, you should always approach the interview with a mind to accept that you might have to encounter a number of no's before you hit the final yes!

While many candidates prepare for the interview right on the morning of the interview day, it is recommended that the process of interview preparation starts early. As the famous saying of John Wooden goes, 'Failing to prepare is preparing to fail', you should take immense care while preparing for your job interview. While you might be preparing for a job interview, it is, in fact, a character preparation – something that will stay with you forever and shape your future in many ways.

Preparing for the Interview

Knowing Yourself – First Step

Interview process is a stressful time, and one of the few times when you can feel completely in control of the flow of the interview is when you talk about yourself. This is something that is completely in your control. Often the degree of interview preparation marks the difference between the successful candidate and the unsuccessful candidate. While some of you might start the interview training process only after the job interview appointment is finalized, it is recommended that the process of preparing for the interview start right during your college days.

Most often, interviewers are amazed and amused at the sort of answers candidates provide to basic questions such as, 'Tell me about yourself.' Before you understand the prospective company, you should evaluate yourself and know what you are willing to offer the employer. Evaluate yourself in terms of your skills, educational qualifications, strengths and weaknesses, and career goals.

Remember that everyone seeking a job is a sort of salesperson. While the usual salesperson tries to sell his products, a candidate for a job interview has to sell his potential to the employer. Since every employer almost always starts the interview process with this simple self-introduction type of question, you should make sure that you prepare for the same in advance. You might find it easier to prepare when you think of the job interview as a performance of sorts. As with any performance, you should ensure that you have enough practice to carry it off well.

Make a list of all your strengths and weaknesses; try to think of examples for each strength and weakness you are planning to quote. Try to list your achievements and interests – make sure at least a few of your interests are work related. You should not memorize all your lines and deliver them like an actor – it might not be natural and it doesn't sound practical as well. They will come out as forced and will be less effective in an interview. Moreover, if you forget what you were planning to say, you are sure to get distracted and lose confidence in yourself. However, you should write down the answers to the questions that you expect to be asked during the interview.

Although you cannot be expected to be able to accurately judge yourself, you should still try interviewing yourself at least a few times in front of the mirror. It is always advisable to record your performance so that you can judge yourself and your voice later. You will also be able to rectify any of your mistakes. Look at how you react to those moments when you are unsure about how to deal with a question.

Take extra caution to analyze your pitch, tone, quality of voice, modulation, gestures and clarity and make necessary alterations to suit those of the interviewer. It is natural that during the interview, your nerves are all jagged and your mind is on the verge of deep freeze, so now is the time to be aware of them, and to think of ways to control your fear and nervousness.

It is always suggested that you run a mental image of yourself and how you want to look on the interview day in your mind before you start your preparations. Try participating in mock interview sessions or ask your trusted friends to simulate an interview session for you. Ask them to ask you typical interview questions and be very critical of your verbal and non-verbal communication. Make sure that they are aware and offer critical opinions on your tone, appearance, body language, behavior, eye contact and more. Be open to receive feedback and make the necessary corrections.

Self- Assessment for Better Performance

Self-assessment is a very important step in preparing for the interview, even though sometimes it is overlooked by many. It might be difficult to make the right career plans for your future, but you can start it by focusing on assessing yourself before jumping into the interview fray.

Self-assessment helps you recognize your strengths that you can emphasize during your interview. You can also identify your weaknesses that can be rectified and downplayed during the interview.

Self-assessment helps you build confidence in yourself. When you deeply delve into your background and history, you will be able to identify those strengths in you that can be contributed to your employer. When you have an understanding about your present skills and career goals, you will be able to answer interview questions in a better manner. Moreover, your answers might seem more natural and forthcoming.

When you undertake a self-assessment session, you are more likely to remember all your achievements and goals. You can use this information and connect it with your job profile and merge it with the requirements of the company.

Once you have undertaken a self-assessment session, you will realize that it is a never-ending process. It not only helps you define your career goals, but also makes it easier for you to have a deeper understanding of your skills, areas to improve and your general attitude. Self-assessment is a crucial part of job interview preparation; it helps you anticipate interviewer questions in advance and helps you handle these questions easily.

You self-assessment questions should include,

- Your qualifications that are related to the position
- Skills you can offer
- Examples from previous jobs
- Greatest accomplishments
- Motivating factors
- Positions interested in
- Expectations from the job
- Your greatest strengths and weaknesses
- Your short term and long term career goals
- The reasons for choosing your major subjects

There are chances that you might find many of these questions to be too simple or easy to answer; however, you might find it easier discussing these questions with your friends but find it very uncomfortable discussing the same things with a recruiter. One of the reasons why most of us have an uneasy feeling discussing topics with a recruiter is we all feel that we are being judged. While this might be partially true, you have to also understand that the there are no right or wrong answers to most questions.

Prep your Body Language

Body language plays an important role in determining how you come across during the interview. When we communicate, non verbal communication has a great impact on the listener more than we actually communicate through words. When we interact with others, we are continuously giving and receiving a number of non-verbal cues.

Non verbal communication can play a major role in personality assessment. It, in fact, helps others learn a little more about you, since most non-verbal messages you send play one of these five roles.

- They can agree to and repeat the message you have made.
- They can contradict the message you have made.
- They can underline a message you have made.
- They can add or improve on the verbal message.
- They can substitute a verbal message.

All non-verbal behaviors – from gestures, our mannerisms, the way we walk, talk, and stand, eye contact – everything tells a little more about us. Although these quirks are natural to a person, we have to learn to keep these communication tools in control if we want to give a positive opinion about us. When you stop talking, it doesn't mean that you have stopped talking; in fact, you are continuously communicating non-verbally. Remember that non-verbal communication accounts for nearly 90% of all the messages you are sending to your listener.

Don't lean, don't slouch, sit straight: A bad posture can be deal breaker, right then and there. Don't ever slouch; it suggests that the person is lazy. Leaning back is considered by many as being disinterested and arrogant, and leaning forward too much is considered a sign of arrogance. According to many experts, you should aim for a more neutral way to sit that is neither threatening nor lazy. Sit upright, slightly leaning to the front – maybe at a 10 to 15 degree angle – towards the interviewer. This shows interest and attention. Sit as if there is a string suspended from the ceiling that is holding your head straight.

Hands communicate too: Most of us unsure as to what to do with our hands during our interview or at any time when we are addressing a crowd. In fact, our hands do a lot of communication on their own, and they can be quite a distractive thing during the interview. You should be able to find a way in which your hands don't come in the way of your interview and yourself. You should note that the minute you start pointing at the interviewer to make a point, or bang the table in aggression, you are not taking your case anywhere.

Let your hands rest loosely on your lap or on the table in front of you. If you don't soon find a place for your hands, you are more likely to see them planting themselves nervously in your pockets, fiddling with your hair, scratching your nose, touching your face,

Fiddling with your hair, neck or face is considered a sign of uncertainty and dishonesty. A number of body language experts agree that touching your nose or lips signals that the person is lying.

Crossed arms or hanging by your sides? This is a question asked by many candidates unsure of how to manage their arms – is it better to cross your arms, hang them by your sides or hold them behind your back? Crossing arms against your chest suggests that you are aggressive or resist change. It signals that you are not open to change, and are not flexible. Folding arms against your chest also shows that you are defensive and are feeling threatened. Holding your arms behind your back is not a natural position as it inhibits free movement of your arms. It makes you appear stiff.

Beware of your feet: The way you rest your feet also tells a lot about you. In fact, when you cross your legs or rest them easily on the floor suggests that you are confident about yourself. Constantly jiggling your feet or moving your legs around too much indicates nervousness; it can be very distracting to the interviewer too. If you rest your ankle on your knee, you are sending a signal that you are arrogant and trying too much to look cool. If you cross your legs too high, you appear defensive.

Eyes tell a thousand tales: It is true that your eyes tell a thousand tales that your mouth might not reveal. One of the first cues that you give about yourself through non-verbal communication is through your eyes. Maintain eye contact throughout the interview session; however, don't try to stare down the interviewer. While it is important to look confident and look at the interviewer in the eye, you really shouldn't continually stare at them. Break away the eye contact every now and then. Looking at someone for extended periods of time makes you look aggressive and creepy – you really don't want to give that image. Imagine being the interviewer and you are looking all over the place. As an interviewer, you will find it difficult to concentrate on the answers provided by the interviewee. You might not believe the answers either.

When you maintain eye contact with the interviewer, you are giving signals that you are attentive and that you are interested in what the interviewer is saying. When you keep darting your eyes from one place to another, you are giving signals that you are dishonest. When you constantly seem distracted or keep moving your eyes in an upward direction, is suggests that you are either lying or trying to be sure of something that you are not. Constantly looking down indicates that you are not confident of yourself.

To nod or not to nod: How much nodding is too much? Nod once or twice when the interviewer is making a strong point you completely agree with. After that, you have to find a center position, hold your head still and stay still. Nodding constantly like a bubble-headed doll is irritating and distracting. Keep your nodding to a bare minimum - at least for the sake of the interviewer!

Dress up for the interview

Everyone gets only one chance to make the first impression. If you dress the part, you are more likely to convince the interviewers that you are perfect for your job. The way you dress, and the way you carry yourself, says a lot about your character and how you might behave if you were to be employed by them. If you want to impress the interviewers and get the job, you should be willing to take some time out to get the right dress and accessories.

- **Bad hygiene is a deal breaker**: Being clean will certainly take you places. Regardless of whether you are going to attend an interview or going out with a couple of friends, you should remember that bad hygiene has the ability to ruin even the world's most expensive clothes. A fresh body and a fresh mind will help you face the interview panel easily. Wash your hands before you attend the interview, especially if you have sweaty and sticky hands. Since you would normally shake at least a few hands, you should make sure that your hands smell and feel nice.

- **Look and Smell nice**: Looking and smelling nice is going to help you feel confident about yourself. While it might be important to smell nice, you should not overwhelm the interviewer with too strong a fragrance. Your face is the first thing that your interviewers are going to notice, so make sure it looks fresh, approachable and professional. A smile is the best makeup you can wear. Make sure that your eye makeup is just enough to accentuate your lashes. A subtle lip shade is perfect, as you don't want to be looking tacky. You might have the best and most colorful collection of eye shadows, but this is not exactly the right time to show your collection or your makeup prowess. Keep the red, blues and the greens safely tucked in your house and try to look like you are going to work and not to a club!

- **Groom yourself:** Pay attention to your hair, as you have to present yourself in a professional manner to the interview panel. Your hair should not be too dry that it looks like natural hay or too greasy that it sticks to the sides of your head like wet paper. Color your hair if you really feel you have to, but avoid bright colors that look like you have lost a bet with your hairdresser. Try to avoid bright colored hair clips and avoid spiking your hair; make sure your hair doesn't distract the attention of the interviewer.
Check your fingernails before entering the interview room. You should have job-ready fingernails at all times. Your prospective employers are likely to notice your fingernails when you extend your hand for your very first handshake. Try to avoid too bright nail colors; always keep your nails short or at least keep them even. If you have the habit of biting your nails, try

to cut your nails short before the interview and resist the temptation of biting your nails while waiting for your turn at the interview.

- **Dress to look the part**: If the interview you are attending is for a career in a professional environment, you should try to look your part. There are certain rules and regulations for presenting yourself in an interview. If you have dressed up sloppily or in a too casual manner, you are sure to stick out from the rest like an odd person out. Check out the culture of the company; if the employees in the company wear casuals every day, it is alright if you attend the interview in a casual manner as well.

  - ○ **Men**: You should dress in a manner that is appropriate to the position applied to. You should not dress up for the job, in fact, you should dress down. If you are unsure as the dress code appropriate for the interview, it is better to go conservative. Men are better off wearing a dark colored, long-sleeved suit. Formal shoes are a must; they help complete the look. A dark colored suit with a light colored shirt, color-coordinated socks and a neat tie is perfect for the job interview.

    Wear something you are comfortable in, not necessarily what you look good in. You are better off buying a new suit if all you have is something you wore on your 15th birthday! Don't wear loud colors; anything bright and flashy should be completely avoided. Your clothes should be neatly washed and pressed.

o **Women**: A suit with a skirt is the right choice for you if you are looking at a formal dress for the interview. A dark colored skirt and a color coordinated blouse is a better choice than a mismatched dress. For a business casual look, you can try wearing a cardigan or a sweater as well. More importantly, make sure you don't wear see through clothes that might divert your interviewer's attention to somewhere you don't want.

Wear something that you are comfortable in – it need not be the latest to hit the fashion scene. The skirt should be of a decent and comfortable height so that you don't have to keep pulling it down during the interview. Shoes can make or mar an interview; make sure you have the right ones for the interview. They should be comfortable to wear, gel well with your clothes, and have one solid color – preferably in black. Make sure that the shoes have reasonably high heels – not too high to hurt your feet and not too low to make you look like you are waddling around in flip flops. Check that your heels do not have anything sticking to them.

- **Accessorize Yourself**: Unlike what you have heard about accessories, they are crucial part of your attire. Wear tasteful, subtle jewelry. Don't wear flashy jewelry, or anything that might set you off like a Bobo the Clown! Anything stylish and elegant like a watch or a scarf that accentuates your costume will do you wonders. A sleek bag or a wallet will do well too.

Know the Company

Researching about the employers is the first chance you get to show your skills as a prospective recruit. Find out as much as you can about the organization, their goals, present market share, the services they provide, their organizational structure, and their recent achievements .

You should learn more about the job you are applying to. Understand the job requirements, and try to match it with your educational qualification and experience. When you know about the employer, you will be better prepared to sync and shape your answers in a way that it you line up your skills to the organizational requirements.

You should know about the job processes of the company, so that you can talk convincingly about how you will be able to fit into their work culture. The best place where you can find authentic information about the company is their official website. Their 'about us' page and social media pages will provide information about their products, services and offers. In addition to knowing what they do, you should also get to know why they are into this business. If they ask you questions about, 'where do you see yourself in the near future,' you will be able to answer it in a better manner if you know where the company is going.

You should also know the culture of the company, their office atmosphere, and dress code if you want to fit into their mold easily. This also helps you dress accordingly as you might stick out like a sore thumb if you come dressed in a three-piece suit and the interviewer is dressed in casuals.

Similarly, you should get to know the company's current events, any new projects they have undertaken, new deals they have signed with other organizations. You should know a little about the organization's CEO, organizational future plans and goals.

Knowing the company will help you answer their questions properly without taking a wild guess. Moreover, you will also be better equipped to ask them educated, clear and relevant questions without embarrassing yourself.

Know the Job Description and Job Requirements

Asking the right questions is as important as giving the right answers. In fact, you should ask yourself some questions about the job before preparing for the interview. Know about the job, its requirements in terms of skill, education, experience and training.

Even if the job description is put up on the company website, it is better to understand it clearly from the HR Manager or job consultant. With the latest job description in hand, you will be better equipped to sync the requirements with your key skills. Before attending the interview, you should get to know the person who is going to interview you and learn a little about them. The best way to do this is to check out their LinkedIn and Facebook profile.

Preparing your Resume

Types of Resumes

A resume is a written document that has a summary of your education, work experience, skills, credentials, and accomplishments. Writing a resume is easier said than done, as an employer forms an opinion about you by looking at your resume. If your resume looks neat, well-structured, devoid of grammatical and spelling mistakes, your employer will assume that you are organized and that you pay attention to detail. There are various types of resumes, however, some of the more popular resume types are:

- **Chronological Resume:**
As the name suggests, a chronological resume starts with your work and education history listed down in order of occurrence. However, your job history is listed down in reverse chronological order – your latest job should appear first. This type of resume is most preferred by recruiters as it is easier for them to see the jobs you have held so far.

- **Functional Resume:**
A functional resume is based on the skills you posses instead of your job history. This type of resume is more preferred if you have a lot of gaps in your

career. This lets you focus on your skill set rather than on your employment history.

• Combination Resume:

A combination resume takes into consideration both your skills and your job experience. In fact, the employment history a person is listed after the skills are mentioned. Moreover, this type of resume lets you highlight your skill that you think are relevant to the job you are currently applying to.

• Targeted Resume:

A targeted resume is customized to meet the specific demands of the current job you are applying to. In fact, it lets you list out all the skills, experience, educational qualifications that are relevant to the current job application.

Points to Include in your Resume

Your resume should have complete information about your education, job experience, skills, additional technical skills, and projects you have undertaken. You have to include information about your accomplishments; make sure that your accomplishments can be linked to the job you are currently applying to. Moreover, your resume should have enough information to spike their interest in you, but not too much that they have nothing to ask you during the interview.

String resumes are those that highlight your achievements, employment history and educational qualifications easily. You should make sure that the same format is being used throughout the resume, as you don't want to have format discrepancies taking the recruiters eyes away from the information. Don't bring in too many colors, non-standard bullets, excessive font variations, - steer away from over-crowding your resume and making it too loud.

Although you are sure of your English and grammar prowess, you should proofread your resume more than a couple of times. Make sure that there are no factual and grammatical errors. If possible, give your resume to any of your friends for editing.

So, what should you include in your resume?

- **Heading**: The resume should have a heading at the top of the sheet. The heading should include your name and contact information. Put the contact information right on top of the page so that recruiters don't have to search through the resume to get your number. Do not put "Resume" as the heading!
- **Objectives**: You should mention your career objectives. Although this section can be omitted, if you plan on including it, make sure that it is kept short and focuses on employer needs.
- **Professional Summary:** This is a short summary of your employment history. You can list out your total experience in the given field and include a word about your highest education qualification.
- **Education:** Make a list of your education in reverse chronological order so that the latest degree you have earned appears first. Make sure to include all your degrees and diplomas.
- **Experience:** Past and current job experiences should be listed in reverse chronological order so that the latest job you had or the present job you are holding is listed first. Make sure that the most relevant job is not buried in less-than significant parts of this section. You can add dates and job titles if you consider them to be very important. Moreover, you should describe the duties, accomplishments, responsibilities, and activities you had undertaken during each of the job tenure.

- **Projects:** This section is very important as it describes the number of projects you had undertaken as a part of your education. You can include information about seminars you have conducted, academic projects and more.
- **References**: Make sure you include a list of references at the end of the resume. The name of the person, their contact number and title has to be included.

What is the Difference between a CV and a Resume

The major difference between a curriculum vitae and a resume is the amount of information provided. A resume, generally, is a one or two pages of your educational, skill and employment summary. It is brief, to the point and concise. It is no more than a couple of pages long, it highlights and summarizes your professional and educational accomplishments and relates it to the job you are currently applying to.

A Curriculum Vitae is more than two pages long as it includes complete educational and professional history. It has a detailed synopsis of your experience and academic history. Moreover, curriculum vitae is mostly used in scientific and academic settings as it provides complete information about your research experience, publications, awards, affiliations, honors, and other presentations. It is applicable when you are applying for grants and scholarships.

Tips from Experts on Preparing a Professional Resume

Writing a resume that stands out from the rest is a sure way of getting noticed and shortlisted. In this ever-changing industry, getting a job is a really difficult, tedious and time consuming task. A resume is one way in which you can create a good first impression on your recruiters. In fact, a well-written resume will surely get your foot in the door. Here are a few tips from experts that will help you cater your resume to meet the high standards required by the industry these days.

Bullet Points: Always stick to bullet points to put your information across to the recruiter. Bullets points are easier to read, makes the whole resume look well-structured, and concise. Don't try using fancy-looking bullets; make your resume look as professional as possible.

Proofread and more proofread: A badly proofread resume will certainly make the recruiter wince and think twice about selecting you. Even though you might have one of the best work experience and educational qualifications, a badly-written resume riddled with grammatical errors is going to find its way into the refuse bin. Make sure you get your resume proofread by your friends or career advice counselors.

Volunteer work: Don't forget to mention the volunteer work you do. You might wonder if it is related to the job you are applying to; however, your volunteer work shows a human side to you that might tilt the minds of the recruiters to your side.

Accomplishments: Make sure you list out all your accomplishments – related and unrelated to work. These accomplishments, from the awards you won for a debate or a painting competition, will make the recruiters look at you as someone who is creative, capable and driven.

Sports: Regardless of whether you play football now, or even swim a hundred meters, make sure your resume points out the fact that you were active in sports. It gives them a picture of someone who is a team player, who is active and takes time out to enjoy other priorities in life. If you were not into sports, then at least mention some of your hobbies.

Failures: This might come as a surprise to many; however, some experts opine that mentioning your failure can swing things in your favor. Employers would like to see that you have tried, failed and also learned a few lessons from your failures. This shows that you are willing to take risks, innovate and learn from your experiences.

Details: You might think that putting in too many details in your resume will make it look cluttered. In fact, recruiters would like to see a few details in your resume, especially details about your previous jobs and responsibilities you undertook. Make sure you have a nice way of telling stories about your previous jobs and accomplishments.

Low-level jobs: Even if you have held a low-level menial job long ago, make sure you mention it. Some of you might think that a part of your previous job experience is not worth mentioning in your resume; however, you will be surprised to know that there are recruiters who will be willing to consider you because of these jobs. Recruiters look at you as someone who is willing to work in a team, challenge themselves, willing to adapt to changes, and roll with the punches.

Travel: Details about your travel experiences might seem out of place in a professional resume, but contrary to popular belief, recruiters are willing to look at candidates who travel a lot, either for education, job, volunteer work or leisure. This shows that the candidates are willing to step out of their comfort zone, look at new experiences in life, and deal with unfamiliar situations in life.

Side projects: Make sure you include details about side projects, seminars and other academic presentations you have participated in. This will give an impression to the recruiters that you are willing to learn from various sources, and have immense practical experience as well.

Social media links: Provide social media links to your prospective employers, as this will present a picture that you are aware of recent technological trends. It will also provide more information about your personal likes and dislikes.

Go for non-traditional resume as well – something like a video resume: Non-traditional resume is gaining importance these days as more and more people are stepping out of their comfort zones. Video resumes are gaining popularity among recruiters too, as it has become a better platform to project you in a good light. It gives a glimpse of your personality, your professional outlook, the way you handle questions, your body language and way you are able to creatively project yourself.

Understanding Interviews

Interviews come in all sizes and shapes, and you should be equipped to handle all types of interviews regardless of your comfort zone. Sometimes you might be facing a panel or interviewers and at other times you might be looking at a solitary interviewer. At times, you would be asked to join a Skype interview or a telephonic session with a recruiter. You should know how to handle each and every type of interview easily.

Telephonic Interview

A telephonic interview is typically a screening interview where the recruiter analysis whether you are fit to attend the second round of interview. Although you are not directly meeting the recruiters, it doesn't mean that you can handle telephonic interview without proper preparations. In fact, you have to invest time and effort to crack the telephonic interview. Some of the key points in acing the telephonic interview are:

- Before the telephonic interview process starts, you should clarify all the details. Since you and your recruiter might not be in the same time zone, you should make sure that the interview time is comfortable for both parties.

- Telephonic interview has a few advantages. You can take help from notes, have a copy of your resume, and have a list of questions to ask the interviewer and more.
- Even though it is a telephonic interview, make sure that you dress the part. This will help you get into the right professional mindset.
- Always make sure that the place you choose to attend the call is calm. The telephone that you are planning to use should be working, the signal should be consistent. Moreover, keep a glass of water handy. As far as possible, attend the interview from a distraction-free location.
- Most of us tend to speak quickly when we are in a telephonic conversation – make sure you slow down a bit.
- You can use gestures while making a point; remember: no one is looking at you. Make a fool of yourself if you want. This will help you put across your ideas in a natural and convincing tone.
- It is always better not to ask questions two seconds into the conversation. Take care not to interject with queries or interrupt your interviewer while they are talking. Give them some time to finish their piece, and then proceed to answer.

- Always end the interview with thanks. Regardless of the fact that you are attending a telephonic interview, keep in mind that the recruiter is still judging you in the same manner.

Skype Interview

Skype video interviews have taken the world of telephonic interviews to the next level; in fact, most multi-national companies prefer an initial Skype interview before conducting the usual one-on-one session with the candidates. This has made it easier for the recruiters to screen the candidates according to the candidate's ability to present themselves. Skype interviews are also useful when the candidate is from a far off location and is unable to travel for the first round of an interview.

Unlike a telephonic interview, a Skype interview is a different ball game altogether.

- You should dress up for the interview in the same manner as you would dress up for a regular interview. You should also make sure that you change your profile picture and user name as well, to something more professional than "SexyBeastOnTheHunt".
- Skype can often bring you many 'can you hear me now?' moments, so ensure that your Internet connection will not let you down at the wrong time.
- Select a nice place to attend the interview. Always clean up the background to something formal and professional.

- You should also take lighting into consideration as you wouldn't want to look washed up or shrouded in shadows during most part of the interview. Choose a location where the lights don't play havoc on your video image.
- Always test the microphone before starting up the interview process. Also, make sure that there are no background noises that are interfering with your communication.
- Keep all necessary attachments such as your resume, portfolio and other supporting documents handy so that you don't have to shuffle around during the interview.
- Needless to say, ask questions at the end of the session and make sure you thank the interviewer.

One on One Interview

One on One interviews are also sometimes referred to as traditional interviews. The format is something like this: you will sit down with an interviewer who will ask you a number of questions designed to help the recruiter decide if you fit the job requirements. Although this format of interviewing sounds simple, it can get pretty tough.

- You will have to go beyond the basics to be able to ace in this interview format. You should be able to present yourself in a professional and positive manner.
- Make sure that your handshake is firm. If you think your hands might get sweaty, keep a dry handkerchief handy. Rub your hands dry and then proceed to the interview room. Practice handshake on a few of your friends to make sure that it is firm. Don't make it too strong – the recruiter should not fear getting a few bones crushed – don't make it too limp – it just sends the wrong message.
- Remember that your non-verbal communication plays a vital role in this interview process.
- Try to break the ice as soon as you enter the interview room. Building rapport with the interviewer is very important.
- The interviewer talks 25% of the time, so listen well; and you control the remaining 75% of the time, so make proper use of it.

- Remember that there is usually a question and answer session at the end of the interview – make use of the time productively. Go prepared with a set of questions to ask.
- Don't discuss about salary during the first round of interview. This is also definitely not the time to talk about rumors you might have heard about the company.
- A warm smile and a good handshake never hurt anybody. Smiling makes you look relaxed. When offered a glass of water to drink, there is no harm in accepting it.

Group Interview

Group interview is the opposite of panel interviews; one interviewer will interview several candidates at once. Group interviews are used for hiring certain positions, and the purpose of group interviews is to shortlist candidates from a group of several candidates. One of the most difficult parts of a group interview is to ensure that you stand out from the rest of the candidates. Although company's use group interviews to expedite the interview process, it might come as a rude shock to any candidate.

- Although you might be feeling nervous, try to smile at every other candidate present in the room. Though you might know or recognize someone in the group, try not to show too much of a shock or astonishment on your face. This will show the interviewer the manner in which you will interact with company team members.
- Don't start sizing up candidates in the room. Try to control the urge; it will start reflecting in your interactions with them.
- Talk to other candidates in the room – even if the interviewer is not present. This is not the time to browse your smartphone or go through your notes. Try making friends with people around you so that when the interviewer walks in, he might notice that you are already interacting with others.

- Try to remember names of other candidates. This will come in handy during the group discussion session. Try to involve others in the discussion and make sure you address others by their names.
- You can build upon the ideas of others but make sure you mention the idea, paraphrase it and then add to it. Don't summarize others' ideas and sell them off as your own – you won't be fooling anyone!
- Speak up with confidence. Regardless of the ideas you put up in the discussion, make sure you put them up in a forceful and purposeful manner. You don't have to bang the table to get your point across; all you have to do is talk in a way that you will be noticed.
- In a group discussion, it is easy to get carried away with what you are going to say next rather than listen to what is being discussed. This is where all the problems start cropping up. If you want to speak something meaningful, you have to make sure that your points are tuned in to the conversation, and are engaged with where the conversation is heading. You should pay attention to the person speaking, and make use of your body language to show that you are very much a part of the conversation.

Interview Formats

Each and every interviewer you meet will have a different manner of interviewing. Regardless of the interviewing style used by the interviewer, you should be well prepared, flexible and confident of success. There are three basic interviewing formats: structured, unstructured and behavioral.

- **Structured Interviews:** Structured interviews appear rigid and formal as the interviewer asks the candidates a specific set of questions. In some case, the answers to the questions might be noted as well.
- **Unstructured Interviews:** Unstructured interviews are more casual and conversational in nature. The interviewer has a set of questions in mind, but asks the questions in a natural and conversational manner. The flow of information is from both the interviewer and interviewee.
- **Behavioral Interviews:** In a Behavioral interview, the interviewer asks a few very pointed questions to elicit responses from you regarding the way in which you handled certain situations in your previous employment or provides you with hypothetical situations to understand the way you would deal with such challenges in the future.

Attending the Interview

Arrive on Time

Interviews, in general, are stressful situations and it is better if you don't make them more stressful to you by arriving late to the interview. It is always better to arrive early than walk in a few minutes late to the interview. Your interviewers would not appreciate anyone walking in late for the interview as, in most cases; your interviewers would be running on a tight schedule. Moreover, if you arrive late, you would be cutting the time allotted to you. In addition to this, another most important point to note is that, if you are late you will be sending a very bad signal to the recruiter about your work ethics and discipline.

Importance of First Impressions

There is a very famous saying, 'You don't get a second chance to make first impressions,' and this is true in almost all the situations. When you are planning to get past an interview session, you are most likely to concentrate on answering tough questions, breaking the tension by providing slightly witty anecdotes, and minding your body language. After all, you have to do everything to get past from 'tell me about yourself' to 'welcome on board.'

Nevertheless, to be able to get to the offer letter, you should first make the right impression. From the moment you walk into the interview room, you should make the right impression. When you first meet a person, he or she will make judgment about you in barely four seconds. Moreover, within the next 30 seconds, he finalizes his opinion about you. Here are a few tips to help you make the right first impression to you future boss.

- **Smile and look like belong:** A little smile and a relaxed appearance will take you places. Keep your head high, smile at the panel present, and say a warm hello. Don't forget the receptionist and the administrative staff – smile and wish them. Sometimes, they also have a say in the recruitment process.
- **Remember names:** Most people tend to forget the names of people because they are busy thinking about what they are going to say next. First, listen to the speaker, try to remember their names and use their name the next time you speak to them.
- **Be interested and engaged in the conversation:** When your recruiter is talking to you, show genuine interest and engage in the interaction.
- **Compliments will be appreciated:** Everyone likes a compliment or two, and

your recruiter is not an exception to this! Be sure to make the compliment a genuine appreciation.

- **Turn about knowledgeable:** You should care enough to do some homework about the organization before you attend the interview. Your recruiters will certainly appreciate your efforts and it will boost your confidence.

Break the Ice

Ice breakers help relieve tension related to interviews. It is very important to have a few ice breaking tips handy which can help you set the tone for the rest of the interview. Moreover, ice breakers help you talk about something that you and your recruiter are fairly comfortable talking about.

- **Let the recruiter start the conversation:** Don't give into the urge to start the conversation. Mostly, the recruiter starts the conversation with a casual and usual question, 'Did you locate the office easily?' Since you already know what the first question is going to be, it is better you come prepared with positive response laced with a touch of humor. Don't provide a long-winded story that provides intricate details about your dreadful search for the office!
- **Make it short and sweet:** Short answers have more power and substance than long winded responses. The ice breaker should not last more

than a few minutes. Remember – traffic and the weather are not examples of ice breakers.

- **Don't bring in politics or dark humor:** Humor has to be used to your advantage. Although humor has the power to relieve tension in the room, see to it that you don't bring in politics into it. Moreover, don't feel obliged to deliver a small stand-up comedy stint either.

Ask Questions

At the end of the interview or the discussion, most interviewers give you the opportunity to ask them questions. When a interviewer asks you if you have any questions to ask, you should never say 'No.' Always remember that this part of the discussion is also a part of the whole interview process and that you are required to ask the recruiter meaningful questions. Make sure you ask intelligent, meaningful and relevant questions, as you will be judged based on the questions you ask too. Even if you have nothing further to ask, at least ask for the interviewer's business card or ask them if they require any more information from you.

Some questions to ask the interviewer:

- How would you describe a normal working day in this position?

- What kind of a formal training program would I be required to undergo?
- What are the department goals?
- What kind of performance review process do you currently have?
- If hired, whom would I be required to report to?
- What is the potential for career advancement?
- Do you source employees from outside or tend to promote from within the organization?
- Do you encourage continuing education?
- What kind of a candidate are you looking for?
- What is the next step in the hiring process?

Preparing to Answer Tough Questions

10 Frequently Asked Interview Questions

There is no sure way to predict the kind of questions the interviewer will ask, so it is better to go prepared for some of the most commonly asked interview questions. Here is a list of ten of the most frequently asked interview questions and tips on answering them correctly.

1. Tell me about yourself:

This is one of the most frequently asked interview questions and you can't be surprised if this is the very first questions the interviewer asks you.

Talk about yourself – give information about your education, career, goals, accomplishments, previous jobs. In addition to this information, also provide examples of traits that describe you the most – hard working, organized, and flexible.

2. Why should we hire you?

This is an open ended question, but make sure you don't ramble on forever. Always make sure that you keep your answers short and concise.

Tell them why you think you fit the description for the job. Tell them the skills and experience you would be able to bring to the position and the organization.

3. What is your greatest strength?

This is another question that can be used to your advantage.

Think about strength or a virtue in you that you are most proud of and that is related to your job performance. It could be a skill or a strength you possess. Talk about it for a minute and then back it up with examples. Make sure that you go prepared to answer such questions.

4. Describe a situation in the past that helped you learn from your mistakes?

This is yet another question that helps you convey the message that you are apt for the job.

Share an experience from which you learnt something good, and if you don't have any good experiences to be shared, you have to create one. Think of a lesson you learnt and then talk about an experience to match that. For example, you could say that you were working on a project with strict deadline. Since you understood the requirements of the project, you were confident that you would be able to complete it with the deadline. Unfortunately, you underestimated the time needed to complete the project. You assumed that there would be no delays from your team members. So, you had to extend your work timings to complete the project on time. You learnt that you should not assume, seek clarifications before commencing on your project and to proactively predict the correct deadline.

5. Is there anything in you that you would like to improve?

This is a good question, as your interviewer wants to hear about your efforts at improving yourself. Ensure that the answer you provide is short.

The best answer to this question is speaking about a weakness that you had such as speaking up in the public or mingling easily with co-workers. Once you have spoken about your weakness, you can talk about how you are working towards improving it and also mention how much of progress you have made.

6. How has your education helped you for this job?

You can talk about your coursework, the internship programs you underwent, the projects you worked on, the workshops and volunteer work you were associated with. You should make sure that you not only provide information about your education and coursework, you should also give examples and link them to the job. For example, you could say that since you organized workshops and volunteer work during your college days, you have learnt to work in a team and lead a team.

7. **What can you tell about your work experience?**

This is where you bring in anecdotes about your past performances in such a manner that the interviewer believes you would be able to deliver the same kind of performance in this job as well.

You should focus on jobs that are related to the present job you are applying to. In addition to this, also mention various skills that are completely unrelated to the present job. This will make the recruiter realize that you will be able to bring in additional skills to the current job. Always substantiate skills with examples of accomplishments to put across the point in a better manner.

8. **Which work environment makes you most productive / or describe your ideal work environment?**

Unlike some of you might assume this is not a trick question at all. In fact, recruiters ask this question just to see if you fit in with their work culture. Moreover, the recruiter is trying to know if you are aware of the work environment in the organization which you are applying to.

You should focus on describing your ideal working environment as something in which you can use your skills and talents. You can, for example, say that the ideal work environment is where team work is encouraged, and where employees are given opportunities to excel.

9. What are your career goals?

This is an important question as the recruiter wants to know if you have a plan for the future.

Since the interviewer wants to see if you have a plan for your future, you should make sure that your answer indicates that you have a plan for the future and that you are already working towards it. You have to indicate that you are goal oriented person who has both short and long term goals. You should show that you have the right initiative and proper planning to achieve your career goals. Make sure that your career goals are in line with the company's processes and future plans.

10. Why would you like to work for our company?

This question is another opportunity presented to you to impress the recruiter by spelling out your skills.

Focus on selling yourself. This is the right time to talk about your strengths, your skills and how well you fit in with the organization. This is also the right time to talk about various other skills you possess about which you haven't been able to discuss.

Smart Answers to Tough Interview Questions

1. What is your greatest weakness?

Tip: Interviewers don't expect you to be perfect (without weaknesses) or expect you to reveal you true weaknesses. Talk about a personal weakness that can be turned around and be made as a professional strength.

"I have this habit of worrying myself over deadlines and targets. I sometimes double-check everything to make sure it is perfect. I don't seem to be able to relax until I get the job done correctly. Although it is good for the completion of the work, I have had to work late in order to finish it to perfection. Off late, I have learnt to dedicate time for cross-referencing and double-checking without extending the deadline. Moreover, I have also learnt to check each section of the work as and when I finish it."

2. What are your salary expectations?

Tip: You probably shouldn't give a number because if you are unsure of their offer, then you might have quoted a lesser amount. Moreover, quoting something exorbitant is also going to be damaging to your needs. So, the best way to deal with such questions is by putting the ball back in their court. If you are attending the interview through a job consultant, you can ask them for a ball park salary that the company is willing to pay, before going for the interview.

"What are you planning to pay the best candidate for this position?" Or, if you are sure of the going price, you can suggest that you would like to accept 25% more than your previous salary.

3. What does success mean to you?

Tip: Don't go overboard with your philosophical viewpoint on what success really means and what a successful life does to you. Keep it purely professional.

"For me, success is based on the short and long term goals I've set for myself. Success is meeting them with aplomb. I evaluate success as meeting the expectations of my supervisors and meeting the deadlines of the clients. Success is working together to completing the organizational goals and targets."

4. Why did you leave your previous job?

Tip: Be honest. If you had any problems in your previous organization, this is the time to come clean about it. If you did not, then simply give a straightforward answer. Don't fiddle around.

"I relocated to this city to stay closer to my parents. Since my previous organization doesn't have a branch here, I had to quit the company."

5. Why did you take so long to find a job?

Tip: Don't get defensive and say that it's not been that very long. Accept that it took time and give proper reasons and explain what you've been doing in that time.

"I realize that it has taken a while to find a job. Since, I have been looking for a senior level position, I found it difficult to find positions that suited my experience and that offered the challenging projects I am interested in. Moreover, during the time I was searching for a job, I completed a short term Project Management course."

6. I have noticed that you worked in ABC and Co for a period of four years, and yet you weren't promoted. Why?

Tip: Don't abuse your old organization or your ex-colleagues. Convey in a subtle manner why you felt you weren't promoted.

"ABC and Co is a wonderful place to work and I immensely enjoyed working there. In fact, the team I was leading contributed greatly to the growth of the organization. However, since ABC and Co was a startup when I joined, promotions were hard to come by. Moreover, once my senior quit the job, we found it very difficult to replace him. That is when ABC and Co hired a new boss, who was keen on bringing his own people to the team instead of promoting from within. I waited for my promotion; however, I sincerely felt that the right time for asking for my promotion had not come. I was quite content with my work and my team's contribution to the overall performance of the organization."

7. Now that you are already in your early forties, why are you willing to start at an entry level position?

Tip: Don't take the comment about your age very seriously. Take time to think about it and answer it with nonchalance.

"I agree that sometimes being in the forties can be disadvantage; however, there comes a time when you have to move few paces backward in order to eventually move forward in your career. Starting at the entry level in this organization would help me learn the business process from the ground up, and better equip me to deal with issues in future. Since the organizations that I've worked in previously are so different from yours, I would like the opportunity to learn the basics of your business. And I am sure the salary cut would be well worth the final results.

8. How many hours a week would you be willing to work and why?

Tip: Don't give a number; your recruiter might think that you would not work beyond the time.

"I usually work for long hours. I like to go the extra mile to make sure that the projects assigned to me come out in a good shape. I extend my working hours depending upon the nature of the project and the deadline. I want the projects offered to us delivered in an impeccable manner.

9. Describe a time when the work load given to you was heavy and talk about how you handled it?

Tip: Accept that workloads become heavy, at times. Speak about how you deal with it by providing examples of the manner in which you have handled them.

"I accept that sometimes workload becomes heavy; in fact, more than usual. However, I have realized that not all the tasks given to you have the same deadlines and not all are mission-critical tasks. So, I have found it easier to deal with heavy workloads by focusing on mission-critical tasks, and prioritizing them. I talk to my supervisors about each task and chalk out a plan to execute each of these tasks."

10. Did you ever make a mistake that cost your company money?

Tip: It is not a good idea to be honest here; although, you can certainly liven up the situation with a witty joke.

"Does asking for the super-costly vodka at the team party count? I guess not! On a serious note, I have not made any mistake that was responsible for a loss for the company."

11.Under what circumstances do you think it is acceptable to break the confidence of someone?

Tip: You might say the truth here; however, you should remember that the recruiter is looking at how well you would suit the organizational goals and is not scoring your ethics.

"I think I would break someone's confidence when I am sure that the person is involved in doing something unethical. If I am sure that confiding about this to someone is going to stop or reduce the impact of the unethical act, I would certainly break the confidence."

12.Why do you consider yourself a leader?

Tip: Reinforce the fact that you consider yourself a leader and give reasons why you think so. Provide examples for each reason you give.

"I consider myself a leader because I have a number of leadership qualities. Although I am an extrovert, I am a rapt listener. I believe that if you listen to people, you get solutions to a lot of interpersonal communication issues. Since, I am a stickler to perfection; I have the qualities to encourage others to finish their work on time and in perfection."

13.Have you taken any unpopular stands?

Tip: Don't say you haven't taken any unpopular stands – it shows lack of self-identity. You would come across as someone who doesn't stand up for themselves.

"I had a situation in my previous company where the distribution of work seemed unequal. Those of us who worked well were always given extra work and strict deadlines. Our team delivered the projects on time and every time. However, things went out of hand when we were asked to work on holidays thrice in a row. That is when I approached my team management to talk about work distribution and also to give us our due for the work already completed."

14. You have changed careers a number of times before, why should I hire you?

Tip: Don't deny the fact that you have changed jobs, and don't say that you regret changing careers. Accept that you have changed course many times but also put it across that you have learnt from these experiences.

"Yes, I have changed careers, but I have learnt quite a lot in every one of the jobs I've held. Moreover, I think I am a better employee because of the diverse experience and skills that I possess. This skill set has made me into a creative person who looks beyond the box for solutions to problems."

15. Don't you think you are overqualified for this job?

Tip: Don't assume that this question is directed at your age.

"I understand that I might be overqualified for this job. But, isn't that just wonderful. I would be able to bring in my experience and qualifications to the job. Moreover, I am a self-starter, I don't require constant monitoring and I am great at interpersonal skills."

16. Where else are you attending interviews?

Tip: Don't deny the fact that you are interviewing elsewhere too.

"I am attending interviews at the top five firms. However, I would like to work here as I think this will provide me an opportunity to learn, and provide me with many roles and responsibilities, unlike bigger companies."

17. If you are not offered promotion, won't you get frustrated?

Tip: Don't vehemently deny the fact that you will be frustrated as any normal person would be. Just make sure you put across the idea that even though you get frustrated, you would be willing to take it in your stride and continue to learn.

"I certainly consider myself as a very ambitious person. Although I am ambitious and would like to win, I am also a very practical person. As much as I enjoy getting promoted, I immensely enjoy learning and growing within my position. I know that different companies have different ways of promoting its people and I am sure that when I exhibit the skills I've learnt, you will keep me motivated for years to come.

18. What would your previous boss or co-workers say about you?

Tip: Don't brag and at the same time don't be too humble and shy.

"I am pretty certain that my co-workers and my boss would have nice things to say about me. My boss would tell you that I was one of the eager and fast learners in my team. I would not hesitate to go the extra mile to get the work done according to client needs. My co-workers would call me an enthusiastic worker who enjoys challenges. They would remember me as someone who loved rolling up the sleeves for work and play."

19. How long will you stay with us?

Tip: Recruiters ask this question just to see if you have any long term plans with them or if you are looking to quit in a couple of years' time.

"I am willing to stay for as long as I can. I am not looking to change jobs often. I am planning to form a career. Moreover, I had stayed in my previous job for more than 3 years. I am sure I can top that here."

20. Would you be willing to relocate?

Tip: Some companies require you to be flexible. If you say you are not willing to relocate, it might become a deal-breaker. However, if you don't want to move, you should unequivocally just say, no.

"No. I am really not interested in relocating right now. However, you never know what tomorrow will bring you."

"Yes. It really doesn't matter where I live as long as I am learning new skills, advancing my career interests. If relocating is a necessary part of the job, then I would be willing to consider it."

21. Talk about a time when your hard work was criticized and tell us about you handled it?

Tip: You have to portray that you are coachable and that you take criticism well.

"During the beginning of my career, I've had one such experience. Although I was new to working, I worked extremely hard to learn the processes. Since, I took a long time to make sure everything was in order; my supervisor criticized my working style. He taught me different methods to get the work done easier. I enjoyed learning new concepts and easier methods of meeting deadlines. I thoroughly enjoyed the learning experience."

22. What is your work style?

Tip: Your work style is the manner in which you prefer working – alone or in a team. It certainly is not your dressing style!

"I am a good team player who enjoys rolling up my sleeves with the rest of the team. I am very comfortable brainstorming, planning strategic solutions together. I am sure that every company is structured around teams and I have the right spirit to work in any team."

23. Talk about a time when you had to confirm with a policy even though you did not agree with it.

Tip: This is a question that can get you into trouble easily. You can't say that you disagreed with a policy and you still continued to confirm to it. It shows you as someone who is unethical.

"I can't think of a situation where I had to confirm to a policy that I did not agree with in the first place. However, I have had concerns over a policy, which I expressed to the concerned employees. I see it as my duty to spot potential issues when I see them before they can turn into problems. However, in the end the final decision belongs to my supervisors."

24. Talk about a time when you felt that you went beyond the call of duty.

Tip: This is the time to brag and not be humble. Combine a story of your work, the actions that you took and the results you achieved.

"There was a time when our team had to complete a series of tasks within a short period of time. I knew we did not have the right resources to complete the task. However, we managed to complete most of the tasks well before the deadline. Unfortunately, something went wrong with our computers and we lost most of the saved data. I volunteered to stay back and get the work completed before the deadline. I received congratulatory notes from both my managers and the clients for my work."

25. Did you ever find it difficult to work with a manager?

Tip: Play it safe. They are looking to know more about you and not your ex-manager. Don't tell anything negative about your manager even if you have had bad experiences. You might play it safe and say you never had anything bad with your manager. However, you could turn around, say yes and give a convincing answer.

"Yes, in fact, I did get off on a bad foot with one of my managers in my very first job. We both had different expectations from one another and since it was my first job, I didn't know whom to approach to clear the air. Finally, we had a talk and the air was cleared. Eventually, he encouraged me to excel in my work and he became a sort of a mentor to me. It seemed communication is the key to all relationships."

Tips to Understand the Mind of the Interviewer

When you are busy preparing for the interview, you should remember that the final call comes from the interviewer. So, it becomes important that you understand the mind of the interviewer to get the dream job. You succeed in a job interview by not convincing the interviewer at the final stages of the interview process. It is about convincing each and every person along the way. The non-interviewers play a major role in you getting shortlisted for the job. Although most of them give you a 'No opinion' rating, it is far better than getting a disapproval rating. One misstep with the receptionist and you might actually find yourself facing a grumpy interviewer. So, make sure you smile and be nice to everyone you meet. Always be on your best behavior and treat everyone with courtesy even if you think they are not going to be a member of the interview process.

Interviewers are more concerned with approving or disapproving you. They can either hire you or not hire you. The person interviewing you has a lot at stake too; his or her reputation is hanging on your candidature. If you have been shortlisted for the second round of interview, you can be sure that the interviewer in the second round is going to judge the first round interviewer's decision.

Be a person that anyone can recommend to others. Think of the interviewer's personality or working style. Ask yourself if the interviewer is willing to hire you immediately or shortlist you or refer you for a second round. Every interviewer has a few hot buttons that you should not interfere with; you will be able to get clues to them during the course of the interview. Every interview and every company is hiring for a different reason and make sure you don't come with the same answers to every question.

Closing the Deal

Thanking the Interviewer

There is no excuse for not thanking the interviewer. It is better you ask for the interviewers' business card and send him/her a letter of appreciation as early as possible. Since we are in the email era, you can shoot the thank you letter as soon as you are able to find time. If you think that the company will recruit very quickly, you should send in your appreciation letter as early as possible – that is before they make their decision.

Proper communication will be appreciated and make sure you make use of the thank you letter. Ensure that the thank you letter is more than just a plain thank you note. Convey to the interviewer your interest in the position and the company. Pick a topic that you discussed during the interview so that the interviewer knows who you are. Review some of the points discussed during the interview so that his/her memory is refreshed. You can also reiterate some of the skills and educational qualifications you possess. You can also talk about any significant qualities in you that you missed mentioning during the personal interview. If you receive an immediate reply, you can be sure that they are interested in you.

Follow-up Communication

Follow-up communication is necessary as it shows your interest in the job and the organization. It is always important that you reply immediately to any of the mails sent by the representatives of the organization. Any delay in communication would be considered as sheer lethargy or disinterest.

Make sure that you get the business cards of your recruiter, and send the right thank you note. Take care to not only use the right tone but also right grammar and spelling. Take extra caution to get the name and spelling of the interviewer right.

Before leaving the interview location, enquire the right persons about the next steps in the selection process. In some cases, the interviewer would spell out the steps in the selection process. If, in case, you don't receive any information, make sure you ask for it.

If you interviewer asks you to call back on Thursday, you better call up on Thursday. Not a day early and certainly not a day late. Failure to call on the stipulated day could prove detrimental to your candidacy. There is nothing wrong in being a little persistent. While some of you might assume that being persistent might make you look desperate, the fact is, recruiters appreciate a bit of persistence. Being persistent doesn't mean you have to keep badgering the recruiter. Decide on the right technique and right amount of aggressiveness depending on the position you are looking for.

Accepting the Offer Letter

Once the company has given you a formal letter of offer, you can choose to either accept it or deny it. However, regardless of your acceptance or denial, you should make sure that you intimate the company in writing.

When you accept the offer letter, it is always better to write a formal letter of acceptance to confirm to the details provided in the offer letter. Before accepting, make sure you read the letter at least a couple of times. You have to be sure about the details of employment provided in the offer letter. Before sending in the acceptance letter, it always better to first acknowledge the offer over the phone. Call the hiring manager and let them know about your intentions to accept the offer. Once you have confirmed your intentions over the phone, it is the time to write a formal letter of acceptance. Make sure that the letter is brief and concise. Don't start rambling about your virtues; it is the time to keep it simple. Your offer letter should contain a formal note of thanks for selecting you and appreciate the opportunity provided to you. Mention the details of employment such as salary, benefits, designation, probation periods, and more. Confirm the date of joining; it is better not to leave it ambiguous. You can use this opportunity to clarify the doubts you might have had and also to inform the company if you are unable to join them on the specified day because of any prior engagement.

Negotiating the Salary

If the company offers a salary which is below your expectations, then you can voice your concern at this stage with confidence. Don't be afraid to ask as no one loses a job offer just because they asked, but do not be too demanding either. Here are a few salary negotiation tips:

- Do your research about the prevailing salary range in the market. Web sites like glassdoor.com and LinkedIn can help you research the compensation levels and perks at your prospective employer. If you're dealing with a recruitment agency, your consultant should be able to advise you on the salary range for the position you're interviewing for.

- Never discuss salary too early in the interview process. Try as much as possible to not quote a number. If the recruiter presses too much, just give a ballpark range as your expectation. This will allow you to negotiate once the offer is made.

- In many cases, the employer will reject your first request for a higher offer. Don't let this deter you. Push back gently, justifying your proposed salary. Explain how the company will benefit from the investment.

- It's easier to negotiate the salary over a face to face meeting rather than on the phone. People feel more of an obligation to other people when they're physically present.

- If the hiring manager finds your salary request to be too high, offer to do a project on a prorated basis. Once you're in the door and showing how good you are, the employer will likely meet your salary request.

- If you're interviewing for other jobs, you might want to tell employers about your offer. This should speed up the interview process. If they know you have another offer, you'll seem more attractive to them, and it might help you negotiate a higher salary.

- If the company won't budge on salary, negotiate other compensation. Ask for things like an extra week of vacation, company car or a flexible schedule. (Maybe you can work four ten-hour days instead of driving to the office five days a week!) Other possible perks include transit passes, educational reimbursement, better health insurance, performance bonuses, or permission to bring your dog to work.

Ideally, both parties in a negotiation should come away from the table feeling that they've won. This is especially true when you're dealing with salary negotiations. You want employers to have good feelings about the price paid for your services so that your working relationship begins on a positive note.

Handling Rejection with Grace

Candidates, often, look at rejection as a disgrace. Being rejected after performing well in a job interview can severely dent a person's confidence. However, since you know that you have given your best, there is certainly nothing wrong with you but the company's needs and your skills do not match. By thinking objectively, you can certainly look at rejection as a learning process. You should have learnt something from the interview; you should have understood your skills better. The first and foremost step is self-assessment – identifying your competencies, your strengths and weaknesses. If you have been rejected just this one time, you can certainly look at rejection as a step towards better employment opportunities. However, if you have been rejected more than a couple of times, then, you should look at where you go wrong, understand your body language and also plan your next steps.

The next step in dealing with rejection is addressing the issues. One of the most common reasons for rejection is the lack of technical knowledge. In fact, the reason for being rejected by one company can be turned around to become the main reason for getting accepted by another company. Remember that rejection is certainly not a feedback and should not be perceived as one.

Never carry the interview rejection baggage around. You have to approach each new job with a fresh mind and perspective. You should start working on tailoring your resume to meet the new needs of the next interview. Learn from the mistakes you made in your last interview since each company and each recruiter will have a different approach towards interviewing and different ideas about an ideal candidate. All you have to do is keep learning from your mistakes and developing your skills and talents to meet the changing needs of the job market.

Bonus Chapter: 12 Hours to Interview Readiness Checklist

09.00 – 10.00 am

- Find out the location of the interview, landmarks near the place. Obtain a detailed map to the location from the company's website or make use of Google Maps. The fact that sometimes these maps are not reliable makes it all more important for you to undertake a dry run.

- Do dry runs to the interview location to know the exact time it would take to reach the destination tomorrow.

- Familiarize with the directions, the route, traffic congestion, and estimate the correct time to reach the place.

- If you don't reach at least 15 minutes before the stipulated interview time, make necessary adjustments and start early.

10.00 – 11.00 am

- Decide on the outfit for tomorrow. Make sure you have everything pressed and ready. If you have favorites, this is the time to take them out.

- Place every single element of the outfit on your bed – from shoes, clothes, watch, accessories, tie and jewelry. Inspect each and every element carefully. Look carefully for rips, tears and spots on your clothes. Polish your shoes to perfection.

- It is always better if you have PLAN B clothing ready that can help you if you have any wardrobe disaster.

11.00 – 12.00 Noon

- Review all your notes once again.

- It is always better to research the company from start once again. You might have missed a few very important points during your first research.

- Go through their interview call letter and see if you have answered all the questions during your mock interview sessions.

12.00 – 1.00 pm

- This is the time for lunch. You really need to relax before the interview day as you don't want to be stressing about the interview way too much. You are also advised to sleep a little as you wouldn't want to look tired.

1.00 – 2.00 pm

- Go through all the questions that you think might be asked during the interview.

- Review all the responses you have planned. Remember all the examples you are planning to quote.

- Think of any redirect questions that might be asked and think of an appropriate response to it.

- You are not supposed to memorize any of the responses but make sure you are comfortable with them.

2.00 – 3.00 pm

- Take some time out to relax with your friends and family.

- It is better to always take your mind off the interview by doing something you enjoy such as cycling, swimming or listening to music.

3.00 – 4.00 pm

- Take a relook at your resume.

- Make sure that your resume doesn't have any grammatical or spelling errors.

- Ensure that you have the right number of copies of the resume as requested by the recruiter.

- If the recruiter has requested you to bring a certain number of resume copies, make sure you carry them. Pack a few photographs, pens, few plain papers with you.

4.00 – 5.00 pm

- Since you have had quite a bit of time to relax, you need to flex your mind muscles a bit more.

- Ask a friend to don the role of a recruiter and conduct a mock interview session.

- You should make this a fully functional interview session. So, dress the part. Remember to smile.

- Your friend should critique your responses, your tone, mannerisms, professional behavior, body language and eye contact.

- Make necessary changes to your approach and try a mock session once again. This time concentrate on your responses to personal and technical questions.

5.00 – 6.00 pm

- Relax for a while – by watching TV or talking to friends. Do anything that you would normally do on a non-interview eve.

6.00 – 7.00 pm

- Perform complete visualization of the interview session.

- Imagine that the interview session was fantastic and that you excelled.

- Imagine the interviewer asking you questions and your responses to them. Imagine yourself being congratulated on your success. Be proud of your achievement. Imagine being confident and sure of yourself.

7.00 – 8.00 pm

- Undertake a final review of your questions.

- Prepare a final checklist of things you have to take to the interview location.

8.00 – 9.00 pm

- This is the time to relax and have a hearty and nutritious meal. Drink lots of water and refreshments.

9.00 – 10.00 pm

- Time to sleep.

- Make sure that you pack your bag with all the things you have to take to the interview.

- Make use of the checklist you have prepared.

7.45 – 8.45 am

- Be relaxed.

- Dress leisurely.

- Eat healthy. Don't eat anything too heavy; it might make you drowsy.

- Go through the checklist once again and reconfirm whether you are carrying all the necessary items.

- Go through your notes once finally.

8.45 – 9.00 am

- Remember to smile and greet everyone present courteously

- Pep up for the interview. This is not the time to take out your notes and review them.

- Small talk with others attending the interview

9.00 am – Interview

All the best!

Conclusion

A usual Interview setting: The all-too-powerful interviewer mercilessly grills the hapless candidate for hours on end, immensely enjoying the nervous looks of the sweating and faltering candidate, prying into the candidate for flaws, spotting weaknesses, somehow turning strengths into weaknesses, and trapping the candidate into saying something that might send him back to the end of the interview race! Ask any candidate about what a job interview feels like and you are more likely to hear something like this. From an interviewees' point of view, this might seem true; however, the fact is that interviewers try desperately to fill the vacant position with the right candidate. When candidates remove fear and apprehension from their psyche, they will be able to better appreciate the importance of the interview process. When they are able to convert the 'interrogation' process into a 'business discussion', they would not just be able to ace the interview but also come out of the whole interview process unscathed.

Thank You!

Thank you for purchasing and downloading this book! I hope the book was able to help you understand everything involved in preparing for your job interview and help you with the resources required to get your dream job!

Finally, if you enjoyed this book, please take the time to share your thoughts and post a review on Amazon. It'd be greatly appreciated!

This feedback will help me to continue writing the kind of books that would give you the maximum value and results. Thank you once again and good luck!

FREE AUDIO BOOK

Don't forget to get access to the Free Audio Book version of Job Interview Preparation by viewing the below link:

http://forms.aweber.com/form/10/1771222810.htm

Format: .mp3

Size: 21.4 mb

Duration: 01:26:29